In You I Trust

Verses, Teachings, and Prayers of
Jewish Tradition to Comfort and Inspire

ISBN: 1-4392-0324-5

ISBN-13: 9781439203248

Visit **www.amazon.com** to order additional copies.

Visit **www.InYouITrust.com** for more information.

In You I Trust

Verses, Teachings, and Prayers of Jewish
Tradition to Comfort and Inspire

Jeffrey B. Alhadeff

For Hayyim ben Alegra
Saludozo

Table of Contents

Translator's Introduction

I am now sitting next to my father in Harborview Hospital located in Seattle, Washington. He fell off his bicycle while riding around "The Lake," as the southern part of Lake Washington is known by the locals. The CAT scan revealed cancer in his lower back. In my attempt to keep my view above the ever-changing reports from doctors and to serve as a merit for my father's speedy and complete recovery, I have decided to translate this little collection of sayings from our prophets, kings, sages, and rabbis.

This collection, in Hebrew known as *Mitsvat HaBitachon*,[i] means a great deal to me. It was a gift from my rabbi, a man of great peace and presence, a man who embodies the positive qualities with which a faith in God can crown a person. He gave the collection to me toward the end of my year of study in Israel after high school. It became a book my wife and I shared together. I have brought it with me nearly every time I went to the hospital to visit my friends and family who have been in need of strength. Everyone I know who has this book has drawn faith and inspiration from these words, culled from biblical, rabbinic, medieval, and contemporary sages who went through difficult times.

May God bless this work to serve as an inspiration to many on the importance of faith, as my father does, as his parents did, and as I and my children may merit to do. My dad is someone who will often explain those times when reason fails by recalling the old Ladino[1] saying, "*El Dio es grande*"—God is great. May God bless my father for many years with life and health in the service of his family, community, and Creator.

A few notes about the introduction:

I should state that I did not finish this work, or even most of the above introduction, while sitting by my dad's bed. He mostly didn't want me typing, but rather talking to friends and family as they visited. My dad is a master of being polite and respectful; I had to temper my more reclusive nature. Fortunately, he was not in the hospital that long. More than a two years have gone by since I started this work. My dad has gone through radiation, chemo, and stem-cell transplants and now is nearly as good as new, thank God, except for the low dose of chemo he needs to take once a week.

In the process of seeing my father get ill when I was still young (twenty-eight years old), I felt myself jump into what seemed my mid-forties. My midlife crisis (perhaps? I hope?) dampened some of my unbridled hopes for

[1] A Romance language derived from Old Spanish spoken by Jews from the Ottoman Empire.

intense spirituality and brought me back to some of the more simple gifts God has given us: family, friends, and faith.

Translating this collection has been incredibly meaningful to me. I felt a number of times that I was shaping clay on a potter's wheel, trying to get the object just right. When the correct translation appeared on a page, a sense of joy would overtake me. Even though I am proficient in Hebrew and it carries a deep meaning for me, it was an overwhelming experience to see the verse or idea captured in my native language.

I have attempted to give a modern and devotional translation to these classic texts. My translations, therefore, have a more poetic feel than other texts. Having said that, in every circumstance I always found support from commentaries for the translation I chose.

I took more liberty when translating the rabbinic writings than I did when translating the verses to account for the unfamiliar sentence structure of these authors. I have attempted to offer their holy words in the most lucid form to my readers, often adding, subtracting, or reorganizing phrases. I have not used brackets to offset my comments from the rabbi's original words, as I do not expect any of my readers will use this translation as a means of studying the original Hebrew. I have also cited the source with the intent that the reader could do further research on the source, and I provide sufficient information in the endnotes to help the reader find the source in the original text. I felt using an exact citation on each page would overly burden the English reader.[ii]

Although the sources apply to both men and women, I translated into the masculine form due to the absence of a non-gender specific pronoun in English and to avoid the awkward he/she construct. I hope all readers will find these texts relevant and meaningful.

Reflecting on the difficulty I had in translating these texts into modern and lucid language, I thought of the Talmudic statement that captures the dilemma I faced on nearly every page: "One who translates a verse literally is misrepresenting the text. But one who adds anything of his own commits a sacrilegious act" (*Kiddushin* 49a). I hope my work will be pleasing in both the eyes of God and humanity.

Jeffrey B. Alhadeff
Seattle, Washington

Verses of Trustⁱⁱⁱ

❦

I

Happy are those who dwell in Your house;
Forever they will praise You, *Selah.*
Psalm 84:5

Happy are the people to have it so:
Happy are the people whose God is the Lord!
Psalm 144:15

The Lord of hosts is with us[iv];
The God of Jacob is our refuge, *Selah.*
Psalm 46:8

Lord of hosts,
Happy is the person who trusts in You.
Psalm 84:13

God who saves!
The King,
Answer us on the day we call out.
Psalm 20:10

You are my hiding place.
You preserve me from distress.
You surround me with songs of deliverance, *Selah*.
Psalm 32:7

Then the offering of Judah and Jerusalem will be pleasant
to God,
As in the days of old,
And as in former years.
Malachi 3:4

Be silent before God;
Wait longingly for Him.
Do not be stirred by a wicked man
Whose way prospers,
Who does the advice of sinners.
Psalm 37:7

God, my Lord,
In You I find shelter.
Save me from all my pursuers and deliver me.
Psalm 7:2

I trust in Your loving kindness;
My heart will rejoice in Your salvation.
I will sing to God: He has been gracious to me.
Psalm 13:6

Protect me, God, for in You I seek shelter.
Psalm 16:1

Display Your wondrous kindness;
Be Savior to those who seek shelter
From people who are fraudulent in their piety.
Psalm 17:7

The king trusts in God;
With the loving kindness of the most High,
He will not be moved.
Psalm 21:8

My God, in You I trust;
Let me not be ashamed,
Let not my enemies triumph over me.
Let none who wait on You be ashamed;
Let those who transgress be ashamed, empty.
Make me to know Your ways, God;
Teach me Your paths.
Lead me in Your truth, and teach me;
You are the God of my salvation;
For You I wait all day.
Remember, God, Your compassion and
Your loving kindness;
They are as old as time.
Remember not the sins of my youth,
Or my transgressions;
According to Your loving kindness remember me for Your
goodness' sake, my God.
Good and upright is God;
Therefore He shows sinners the path.
He guides the humble in judgment;
He teaches the humble His way.
All the paths of God are kindness and truth
To those who guard His covenant and
His testimonies.
Enhance your reputation, God, pardon my iniquity;
For it is great.
He who fears God
Will be shown the path to choose.
His soul will abide in prosperity;
His children will inherit the earth.
The counsel of God is with those who fear Him;
To them He makes known His covenant.

My eyes are always toward God;
He will free my feet from the net.
Turn to me, and be gracious to me,
For I am desolate and afflicted.
The troubles of my heart are enlarged;
Bring me out of my distresses!
Look upon my affliction and my pain;
Forgive all my sins.
Consider my enemies;
They are many.
They hate me with a cruel hatred.
Keep my soul, and save me;
Let me not be ashamed;
For I have sought shelter in You.
Let integrity and uprightness guard me;
I hope in You.
Redeem Israel, God,
Out of all its troubles.
Psalm 25

II

God is my light and my salvation,
Whom should I fear?
God is the stronghold of my life,
Whom should I dread?
When evil men assail me to consume my body,
My foes and enemies rise against me,
It is they who stumble and fall.
Should an army besiege me,
My heart will not fear;
Should a war beset me,
In this[v] I will trust.
One thing I requested of God,
And it is what I will ask:
To live in the house of God all the days of my life,
To gaze upon the beauty of God,
To encounter Him in His temple.
He will hide me in His shelter on an evil day.
Under the cover of His tent will He conceal me;
On top a rock, He will raise me.

Now my head is raised high above my enemies who
surround me;
I will offer, in His tent, sacrifices with joy;
I will sing, I will make music to God.
God, hear my voice when I cry aloud;
Love me, and answer me.
Of You my heart told me: "Seek My presence!"
Your presence, God, I seek.
Do not hide Your presence from me;
Do not repel Your servant in anger;
You have been my help.
Do not abandon me, do not forsake me,
God of my salvation.
Though my father and my mother abandon me,
God will gather me in.
Teach me Your way, God,
Lead me on the path of integrity
Because of my suspicious foes.
Do not subject me to the will of my enemies;
False witnesses have risen against me,
They breathe out violence.
Had I not believed that I would see the goodness of God
in the land of the living...
Hope in God;
Be courageous,
He will strengthen your heart.
Hope in God.
Psalm 27

God is my strength and my shield;
My heart trusts in Him; I was helped.
My heart rejoices:
With song I will praise Him.
Psalm 28:7

In you, God, I take refuge;
Never let me be ashamed;
Save me in Your righteousness.
Remove me from the net laid secretly for me;
You are my stronghold.
Do not deliver me into the hand of the enemy;
Let my feet stand securely.
For I have heard the whisperings of many;
Treachery surrounds me;
Together they scheme against me,
Plotting to take my life.
But I trust in You, God;
I have said, "You are my God."
My fate is in your hand;
Save me from the grip of my enemies and pursuers.
Be courageous,
He will strengthen your heart,
All who hope in God.
Psalm 31:2, 5, 9, 14–16, 25

God annuls the plans of nations;
He thwarts the intents of people.
God's plan endures forever,
His heart's intent from generation to generation.
Kings are not saved by a great army;
A hero is not rescued by great strength.
A horse is a false hope for salvation;
Even in its great power it cannot save.
Truly,
The eye of God focuses on those who fear Him,
On those who hope for His kindness;
To save their soul from death,
To keep them alive in famine.
Our soul longs for God;
He is our help and shield.
In Him our hearts rejoice;
Since in His holy name we trust.
Let your kindness, God, be on us,
As we have put our hope in You.
Psalm 33:10, 11, 16–22

We hear with our own ears, God,
Our fathers have told us,
The deed You performed in their time,
In days of old.
With Your hand You drove out nations,
And planted them;
You afflicted the people, and cast them out.
It was not with their sword that they inherited the land,
Their own arm did not bring them victory;
But Your right hand, Your arm,
And the light of your presence,
For You favored them.
You are my King, God;
Decree salvation for Jacob.
Through You we gore our enemies;
Through Your name we will trample our adversaries.
I will not trust in my bow,
My sword will not save me.
You have saved us from our enemies,
And shamed those who hate us.
In God we glory all day,
We praise Your name forever. *Selah.*
Arise, help us,
Redeem us as befits Your kindness.
Psalm 44:2–9, 27

III

Cast your burden on God and He will sustain you;
He will never let the righteous falter.
Psalm 55:23

Be compassionate to me, God,
For men long to swallow me;
All day warriors oppress me.
My enemies daily long to swallow me;
Many fight against me, Exalted One.
When I am afraid, I trust in You.
In God, whose word I praise,
In God I trust;
I will not fear.
What can flesh do to me?
You have rescued my soul from death,
Even my feet from stumbling,
That I may walk before God in the light of life.
Psalm 56:2–5, 14

Be compassionate to me, God,
Be compassionate to me,
For in You my soul takes shelter;
In the shadow of Your wings I will take refuge,
Until devastation has passed.
Psalm 57:2

You are my shelter,
A tower of strength against the enemy.
Psalm 61:4

For God alone my soul waits quietly;
My salvation comes from Him.
He alone is my rock, my salvation,
My fortress:
I will not severely stumble.
For God alone my soul waits quietly;
My hope is from Him.
He alone is my rock, my salvation,
My haven: I will not stumble.
With God is my salvation, my glory;
My rock of strength.
In God is my shelter.
Trust in Him at all times;
People, pour out your heart before Him;
God is our refuge. *Selah.*
Commoners are a mere breath,
Royalty, an illusion;
Place them on a scale,
They are lighter than a breath.
Do not trust in oppression,
Or put false hope in robbery;
If riches prosper,
Pay it no attention.
Psalm 62:2–3, 6–11

IV

I declare on God's behalf,
Who is my refuge and my fortress,
My God, Whom I trust,
He will save you from the fowler's trap,
From the destructive plague.
He will cover you with His feathers,
Beneath His wings you will find refuge;
His truth is a shield and armor.
You will not fear the terror of night,
The arrow that flies by day,
The plague that stalks in gloom,
Or the destroyer that ravages at noon.
A thousand may fall to your left,
Ten thousand to your right,
But they will not draw near to you.
Psalm 91:2–7

He is not afraid of evil tidings;
His heart is confident,
He trusts in God.
His heart is resolute;
He is not afraid,
Even as he views his tormentors.
Psalm 112:7, 8

Israel trusts in God;
He is their help and shield.
Psalm 115:9

God is with me;
I have no fear;
What can man do to me?
God is with me as my helper;
I can stare at those who hate me.
It is better to take refuge in God,
Than to rely on mortals.
It is better to take refuge in God,
Than to rely on nobles.
Psalm 118:5–9

You may say to yourself,
"My own power and the might of my own hand
Has won me this wealth."
Then, remember God, your Lord;
He gives you the power to earn wealth,
In fulfillment of the covenant that He made on
Oath with your fathers,
As is still the case.
Deuteronomy 8:17, 18

Trust in God with your whole heart;
Do not rely on your own understanding.
In all your ways, know Him;
And He, He will make smooth your paths.
Do not be wise in your own eyes;
Fear God, shun evil.
Proverbs 3:5, 6

One who is adept in a matter will prosper;
Happy is one who trusts in God.
Proverbs 16:20

Many plans are in a man's mind;
Yet it is the counsel of God that prevails.
Proverbs 19:21

A greedy person provokes quarrels,
He who trusts in God will have abundance.
He who trusts his passions is a fool;
He who journeys with wisdom will be saved.
Proverbs 28:25–26

A man's fears become his trap;
He who trusts in God will be secure.
Proverbs 29:25

V

Behold, God is my salvation;
I will trust, and not fear.
God is my strength, my song:
He has become my salvation.
Isaiah 12:2

Trust in God forever and ever;
In God is the strength of all worlds.
Isaiah 26:4

Alas, those who go down to Egypt for help,
Depend on horses,
And trust in chariots, because they are many;
And in horsemen, because they are very strong;
Yet they look not to the Holy One of Israel,
Nor do they seek God!
Isaiah 31:1

God is our judge;
God is our prince;
God is our king;
He will save us.
Isaiah 33:22

Those who trust in God will renew their strength;
They will grow wings as eagles;
They will run, and not tire;
They will walk, and not faint.
Isaiah 40:31

Turn to Me and be saved,
All the ends of the earth;
I am God;
There is no one else.
Isaiah 45:22

VI

God declares:
Cursed is a man who trusts in mortals,
Who makes mere flesh his strength,
Whose heart turns away from God.
He is like a lone tree in the desert,
Who will not see when good comes;
But inhabits the parched places of the wilderness,
In an uninhabited salt land.
Blessed is the man who trusts in God,
Whose hope is God.
For he will be like a tree planted by waters,
Spreading out its roots by a brook.
It will not sense when heat comes,
Its leaves will always be green;
It will not be anxious in a year of drought,
Nor will it ever cease yielding fruit.
Jeremiah 17:5–8

"I will rescue you;
You will not fall by the sword.
Your life will be your remnant of the war;
Since you trusted Me,"
Declares God.
Jeremiah 39:18

You, return to your God.
Practice love and justice,
And constantly trust in God.
Hosea 12:7

The remnant of Jacob will be,
In the midst of many peoples,
Like dew from God,
Like raindrops on grass,
Which do not need any man,
Or rely on any mortal.
Micah 5:6

God is good,
A fortress on a day of distress;
He is mindful of those who find refuge with Him.
Nachum 1:7

Exploring Trust

❧

To trust in God is to know in one's heart that all is in the control of Heaven. It is in God's hands to change nature and to alter fortune; nothing large or small stops God from saving. Even if trouble is near, salvation is soon to follow, since He is able to do anything and nothing can stop what He plans. One should trust in God in every trouble and every dark moment. One should know that God can save, and His salvation comes in the blink of an eye. Therefore one should trust in His salvation, even if a sword is placed on one's neck. As it says, "Though He slay me, I will trust in Him" (Job 13:15).

Further, "Trust in Him at all times" (Psalm 62:9), meaning, trust in Him at every time, even when trouble is near and you do not know how you will be saved from it.
Rabbenu Yonah[vi]

It is conceivable to find a person who trusts in God in general, who believes with a complete faith that He is able to do anything, and yet does not turn his attention to trusting God in the details of his life. He remembers God when some great event occurs, like departing on the sea or when traveling a distance, yet does not do so when some small need arises, like traveling to a nearby city. This level of conduct is deficient in the responsibility to serve God.

Full, complete trust in God is that one should remember God in all of his actions. He should know that each act's success is not in his control, but is up to His will. He should consider that harm could befall him even as he travels to a nearby place were it not for God guarding him.

If, perhaps, the act that he set upon was not successful, whether it was significant or minor, he should trust in God always. The reward for the trust he displayed will be greater than any benefit that could have come to him if the act was successful. If the act is successful, then he will have merited having both.

Rabbenu Bachya[vii]

A person who is truly strong in his faith will not only serve God when his life is calm and quiet or when his deeds are successful; yet even when difficult days arise and times of poverty follow him, he should not depart from his simple faith of earlier days. This is the test that a righteous person will go through to see if he is serving God out of love. When many difficulties come to him, he should strengthen himself in His stronghold. His heart should not wane; he should continue to trust in God at all times.

When a person is in peaceful, quiet, successful times, he should not say that it is his might and his strength that brought about this success, but recognize that everything comes from God. He should ask God always to be good to him, and when a difficult time arises he should strengthen himself and trust that God will bring him from sorrow to salvation and that God will bring him peace. This is what the Psalmist intended: "Trust in Him at all times" (62:9), meaning at a time of success and a time of sorrow. "People, pour out your hearts before Him; God is our refuge. *Selah*."
Sefer HaIkkarim[viii]

The expectation that one has for something that will certainly happen, like the rising of the sun, does not worry a person, but makes him happy, in that he is able to measure when that desired good will arrive. So too, it is appropriate for a person to trust in God with a complete faith, that He will fill his desire without a doubt, since He has the ability to do anything, and nothing is able to stop Him. A person should not be like one who is in doubt if something will happen or will not happen; but with a complete faith he will feel encouraged and joyful.

Ibid.[ix]

The students of the Vilna Gaon asked him, "What is one's responsibility in trusting in God?" He answered them, "King David has already explained it for us in Psalms: 'I have taught myself to be content, like a nursing child with its mother, like a suckling is my soul' (131:2), meaning, just as a nursing child eats from his mother's breast until he is satisfied and is not concerned if there will be more milk later when he is hungry, so too, should one's soul not worry what will be later today or tomorrow."
Vilna Gaon[x]

Trust in God and do good.
Dwell in the land and shepherd faith.
Psalm 37:3

The verse starts by saying, "trust in God" and after states, "and do good." That is to say, a person should trust in God that He will help you do His will. "And do good"—chase after His will and attempt to do it; do not be disheartened by your own limitations because He will help you and support you. "Trust in God and do good," then, "dwell in the land and shepherd faith."
Ramban[xi]

Further, "Trust in God and do good" meaning, even if you are not in possession of good deeds and you know yourself to be a wicked person, nevertheless, trust in God since He is fully compassionate and will have compassion on you: "His compassion is for all His works" (Psalm 145:9). Therefore, first "trust in God" whether you are righteous or wicked, and then "do good" when you see that God has been compassionate to you and fulfilled your wishes.
Ibid

It is written, "Many pains befall an evil person; yet one who trusts in God is surrounded by kindness" (Psalm 32:10). Rabbi Eliezer and Rabbi Tanchum said in the name of Rabbi Yirmiah, "Even a wicked person who trusts in God will be surrounded by kindness."
Yalkut Shimoni

It is written, "One who trusts in God is surrounded by kindness" (Psalm 32:1). Meaning, even if one is not worthy of it on his own merits, it is the nature of trusting to draw undeserved kindness for those who trust in God.

Sefer HaIkarim[xii]

Hope is an essential element a faithful person must have to draw kindness from God onto himself. Having hope in God's kindness is the choicest way of serving God. One may think that he is not worthy of God performing an undeserved kindness for him; consequently he does not hope in God fully. Then, the kindness does not arrive. If he had hoped fully in God's kindness, God would have freely given it. Kindness is not withheld by God: He always wants to benefit those who hope in Him appropriately. As it says, "God desires those who fear Him, those who hope for His kindness" (Psalm 147:11).

Ibid.[xiii]

Hope in God that He will straighten your way in His kindness and save you from a path that is wrong; He will choose for you that which is good and pleasing to Him. This happens when one chooses to do good and abhor evil. Do not give up hope of trusting in God due to your sins, since God's providence is drawn to those who hope in His kindness, not to those who hope in God due to their reward. If your troubles continue, even if they be many and evil, continue in your simplicity, strengthen your heart, and hope in God. There is nothing that can stop God from giving you your wishes and granting your desire. His ability is without limit; God can save you from trouble and bring you to salvation. In His limitless kindness, continue to hope in God.

Ibid.[xiv]

God is our refuge and stronghold,
Our help in danger, very near.
Therefore we are not afraid,
Though the earth reels,
The mountains topple into the sea—
Its waters rage and foam;
In its swell mountains quake. *Selah.*
Psalm 46:2–3

This demonstrates how great the responsibility is to trust in God. One would not be afraid or worried even during a difficult time.
Mitsvat HaBitachon[xv]

I have laid down and slept,
I rose since God supports me.
Psalm 3:6

This describes the extent that one must trust in God;
Even during one's greatest troubles he can sleep securely
and rise with his faith.
Mitsvat HaBitachon[xvi]

One who trusts in God is surrounded by kindness.
Psalm 32:1

The opposite is also true: if one is constantly nervous of God's aspect of judgment or punishments, then he attaches himself to judgments, God forbid, as the verse says, "That which you fear I will bring to you" (Isaiah 66:4). Wherever a person's thoughts are, that is where he is. If he thinks about judgments, he attaches himself to judgments. When he trusts in God's kindness, there his soul attaches: kindness will then surround him as he insulates himself in God, may He be blessed.
Magid of Mezritch[xvii]

A man's fears become his trap,
He who trusts in God will be safeguarded.
Proverbs 29:25

The fear that a person has of other people is a great sin and places a trap for him. It can cause the enemy or trouble to approach even closer. "He who trusts in God is safeguarded" from the trouble in the merit of his trust, even if it would have been fitting for the trouble to come.
Rabbenu Yonah

Rabbi Yehudah opened with the following:

> Trust in God and do good
> Dwell in the land and shepherd faith.
> *Psalm 37:3*

A person should always be careful with his Master and attach himself with sublime faith in order to be complete with his Master. Being complete with his Master, no embarrassment can befall him from anything in the world.
Zohar[xviii]

Faith and Trust

Faith and trust are two concepts that are interrelated yet not completely interdependent. Faith precedes trust, yet does not need trust in order for it to exist. Trust, on the other hand, cannot exist without faith. Anyone who can call themselves "one who trusts" is also one who has faith. Yet one who has faith does not necessarily possess trust.

Faith is like a tree; trust is like the fruit. The fruit is evidence that there was a tree that grew it. A tree does not necessarily indicate any fruit: there are trees that do not produce any fruit.

Since it is possible to be one who has faith yet does not have trust, and impossible to have trust without faith, the scriptures always stress the importance of trust over faith.

Ramban[xix]

Dwell in the land and shepherd [*ureh*] faith.
Psalm 37:3

A person might think that they do not have religious obligations when pursuing their business. Therefore, the verse states, "Dwell in the land" when involved in your temporal affairs, and "shepherd [*ureh*] faith"—do not remove yourself from doing acts of goodness even for a moment.

The word *ureh* has an additional meaning, as in the verse, "You must love your neighbor [*ReEcha*] as yourself" (Leviticus 19:18). The meaning of the verse in Psalms can then be understood as, "Dwell in the land and become neighborly with faith." Join yourself with faith in all that you do, as the prophet Habakkuk stated, "A righteous person lives with faith" (2:4).
Ibid.

The Power of Trust

☙☙

God said, "Trust in My name and it will support you." Where did God say this? From the verse, "Trust in the name of God and rely on your God" (Isaiah 3:10).

"Why," God continued, "should a person trust in Me? All who trust in My reputation, I make successful. That is what I did for Chananiah, Mishael, and Azariah, who trusted in Me, and I saved them.

"Indeed, Nebuchadnezzar admitted this when he said, 'Blessed is the God of Shadrach, Meshach and Eved Nego[2], who sent His angel and saved His servants who desired Him' (Daniel 3:28).

"Daniel also was rescued from the den since he trusted in Me: 'Daniel was brought up out of the den; no injury was found on him since he trusted in his God' (Daniel 6:24)."

King David reflected, "If this is the nature of trusting in You, that all who trust in You, You save: I, too, will trust in You."
Midrash[xx]

---

[2] Aramaic names of Chananiah, Meshael, and Azariah.

One who contemplates a matter will attain success,
Happy is one who trusts in God.
Proverbs 16:20

This verse instructs us that a person must plan how to accomplish a given matter. If he does so and is successful, then, "Happy is one who trusts in God." When your plans are successful, do not attribute the success to your plans; rather, consider how everything is in God's control, and it is He who brought your hopes to fruition.
Rabbenu Bachya[xxi]

One who contemplates a matter will attain success,
Happy is one who trusts in God.
Proverbs 16:20

After you have made your contemplations, do not rely
on them; rather, rely on compassion from Heaven. Then,
even when your mind tells you that you are not able to
find a solution, continue to trust in God. Such a person
is truly happy.
Rabbenu Yonah[xxii]

One who trusts in God will not mourn over the denial of his request, nor will he be sad when his beloved falls ill. He will not hoard his treasures and will not seek more than his daily needs, or be concerned about tomorrow; no one knows when their last day is. Trust in God to lengthen your days and provide your needs.

Chovot HaLevavot[xxiii]

Trust and Action

Know that the obligation to trust does not prohibit a person from making plans and taking action; and making plans and taking action is in no way contradictory to the obligation to trust.
Mitsvat HaBitachon[xxiv]

No wisdom, no understanding, and no council
Can prevail against God.
A horse is prepared for the day of battle;
But salvation comes from God.
Proverbs 21:30–31

Wisdom, understanding, and council have no ability to negate that which God has decreed: "If God does not build the house, the laborers toil in vain" (Psalm 127:1).

"A horse is prepared for the day of battle." A person is responsible to guard himself and prepare weapons for battle; and God, He should be blessed, will have compassion according to His will.
Rabbenu Yonah

A person must prepare in accordance with the rules of nature all that is in his ability. If he goes into battle, he must prepare weapons, a horse and chariot; if he does not prepare, he will be handed over to his enemies. Or, if one is ill, he must prepare remedies and medications; he must eat foods that will be beneficial for his health and refrain from unhealthy foods.

Yet, after doing all that is in his ability, he should not rely on his plans or on his efforts, but on God. Since the results are entirely up to God, a person could be perfectly prepared for battle and still lose. A person may not follow any of the medical advice and still be healed. Healing does not come from medication, but from God, "Who heals the brokenhearted and tends to their wounds" (Psalm 147:3). "God does not desire the strength of horses, He does not want the speed of man. God wants those who fear Him; those who hope for His kindness" (Psalm 147:10–11). "The king is not saved with his large army, the hero does not escape due to his great strength. A horse is a false hope for salvation, with its great strength it will still not save. God's eye is turned towards those who fear Him, those who hope in His kindness: to save their souls from death, and sustain them during a famine" (Psalm 33:16–19).
Rabbenu Bachya[xxv]

Rabbi Yossi stated, "Come and understand the difference between one who places the Holy One, blessed is He, as his advocate, to one who places a mortal as his advocate. For the latter, not only are his needs not met, he is considered cursed:

'Cursed is a man who trusts in mortals, who makes mere flesh his strength, whose heart turns away from God. He is like a lone tree in the desert that will not see when good comes; but inhabits the parched places of the wilderness, in an uninhabited salt land' (Jeremiah 17:5–6)."

"One who makes God his advocate, not only are his needs met, he is considered blessed: 'Blessed is the man who trusts in God, whose hope is God. For he will be like a tree planted by waters, spreading out its roots by a brook. It does not sense when heat comes, its leaves will always be green; it will not be anxious in year of drought, nor will it ever cease yielding fruit' (ibid., 17:7–8)."

Midrash HaGadol[xxvi]

Woe, Assyria,
Rod of my wrath,
My fury is a staff in their hand.
Isaiah 10:5

Does an axe glorify itself over him who hews with
it? The saw magnify itself over him who wields it?
As though the rod raised he who lifted it; as if the
staff lifted the man!
Isaiah 10:15

The prophet compares man to an axe: just as the axe's
actions do not come from itself but from the one who
hews with it, so too, a person's actions do not generate
from himself but from God. A person is only like a rod in
the hand of the One who lifts it.
Rabbenu Bachya[xxvii]

When a person acquires any wealth or possession, he needs to give thanks to the Holy One, blessed is He, for this gift. It is appropriate for him to say the following, "I give thanks to You, my God, God of my fathers, for giving me this wealth (or possession)."

Even if a person's livelihood comes from another person, he should not place his trust in that person. He should place the root of his trust, from the depth of his heart, in the Creator, He should be blessed.
Orchot Tzadikim[xxviii]

Everything that comes to a person, be it from his parents or family members or close friends, it is all truly from God. This is seen from the Zohar's comment on the verse from Psalms: "Happy is the one who the God of Jacob is his help" (146:5). Why does the verse state specifically the God of Jacob, why not the God of Abraham or the God of Isaac? Jacob—who did not desire the protection of his father or mother when he was running away from his brother and went in solitude without any money, who said of himself, "With my staff I crossed the Jordan" (Genesis 32:10). He only desired God, as he said, "If God will be with me, guard me on this journey I am pursuing; if He gives me bread to eat and clothes to wear, and if I return to my father's house in peace" (Genesis 29:20). All that Jacob asked, God granted.

Zohar[xxix]

I am greatly astonished at one who gives his friend something that was decreed by the Creator that this person should have, and afterwards, the benefactor asks to be appreciated for what he did. Even more astonishing is a person who receives his salary from another—the recipient is expected to submit, appease, and praise his employer.

Chovot HaLevavot

When a person sees himself successful, understanding, and wise, he should not congratulate himself for his understanding. He should trust in God in all of his affairs, and pray to Him. This is what the verse means when it says, "Trust to God with all your heart" (Proverbs 3:5), meaning, do not consider at all that which you have acquired through your wisdom, only trust in God. That is the meaning of "with all your heart." Do not place into two categories His glory and your wisdom and understanding. There is only God; from Him you receive everything.
Meiri

A person should not think, *I will trust in God, yet I am required to rely on my intelligence.* To counter this idea, the verse states, "Do not rest on your understanding" (Proverbs 3:5). Even resting a little is not acceptable; trust in God with all your heart.

Vilna Gaon[xxx]

When a person perceives with his mind and understanding that a pursuit will be fulfilled through calculations and predictions, do not trust on these predictions since everything is in the hands of heaven. As the verse states, "Who turns sages back, makes their knowledge nonsense" (Isaiah 44:25). Also, "Many plans are in a man's mind; yet it is the counsel of God that prevails" (Proverbs 19:21). Also, "If God does not build the house, the laborers toil in vain. If God does not guard the city, the watchman keeps vigil in vain" (Psalms 127:1). Further, "The race is not won by the swift, or the war by the mighty. Bread is not won by the wise, or wealth by the understanding, or favor by the cultured" (Ecclesiastes 9:11). Finally, "A man arranges his thoughts; it is God who fulfills his speech" (Proverbs 16:1). If God is the one who fulfills a person's speech, how much more so are a person's actions dependent on God!

Rabbenu Yonah

A man arranges his thoughts; it is God who fulfills his speech.

Proverbs 16:1

Know that everything is from the Holy One, blessed is He. A person only has power of thought or speech because of God.

Midrash[xxxi]

A person needs to meditate on his affairs and perceive God's providence for each and every event. Through this reflection, a person's trust will grow. This is the lesson of the verse, "Taste and perceive, God is good; fortunate is the man who finds shelter in Him" (Psalm 34:9).

Shem Olam

Trust and Well-Being

☙❧

In the issues of health and illness, a person should trust in the Holy One, blessed is He, and seek to find cures according to the nature of the illness. This ability to heal is given to doctors: "The healer will heal" (Exodus 21:19). Yet, do not trust in the medication, since the medications have the ability to heal only by the will of God. When a person trusts that God can heal, with proper medicines or without, He will heal him. "He gave an order, healing them; delivered them from the pits of death" (Psalm 107:20).

Chovot HaLevavot[xxxii]

The Torah grants permission to doctors to heal. Healing a person fulfills the positive commandment of saving a person's life. If a person who can heal another does not attempt to, he is considered as a murderer.
Shulchan Arukh

This passage is difficult to understand. If indeed it is a positive commandment to heal a person, why did the above passage begin with "grants permission"? It should read, "The Torah obligates a doctor to heal."

Rather, it should be understood as follows: true healing comes by requesting mercy from Heaven, as stated, "I strike ill; I heal" (Deuteronomy 32:39). Yet, one does not usually merit such clear Divine Providence, so a person needs to take medications and treatment and God will grant permission to the doctors that their efforts should be successful. Once a person has become ill, doctors have an obligation to practice medicine to attempt to heal him.
Turei Zahav[xxxiii]

The trust that everyone must possess is that it should be firm in one's faith and clear in his heart that natural causes and means of healing are entirely up to Divine Providence for each and every individual, at every moment and in every situation. Medicines and natural cause and effect are entirely dependent on His will. It is by His command that they are helpful to most people most of the time.

Rabbi Avraham ben HaRambam

If a scorpion stings you or a snake bites you, do not only take the medicine, but trust in God that the medicine will heal you. In His hand is the soul of every living thing; He brings death and brings life. Since He gave you this punishment and the ability to have a cure, trust that He will heal you in His compassion, as He has afflicted you with kindness. Yet, if you should be in a place where there is no cure available, for example, in the desert, or if you have an intestinal illness for which there is no doctor or medicine, then trust is all that remains for you.
Ibid.

In conclusion, a person is obligated to be responsible and find cures for his illness; yet he must trust in God that He will make his endeavors successful. This is what our sages intended when they stated, "One who goes to have a procedure should state the following: 'May it be Your will, God and God of my ancestors, that this procedure should heal me'" (Berachot 60a). This statement must be reviewed and repeated in a person's mind many times until it is so clear to him that this insight will not leave him. When one reaches this level of trust, he will not feel overly burdened to find the finest medical facilities, but will rely on the words of our sages, "Minimize your worldly affairs, and study Torah" (Avot 4:10).

Ibid.

Trust and Sustenance

Blessed is God,
Day by day He supports us.
God, our deliverance. *Selah.*
Psalm 60:20

Each and every day, He supports us and carries His blessings and goodness to us. It must enter into each person's heart, with total trust, that He will provide for every single day all that we need. Never worry from one day what will be on the next.
Mitsvat HaBitachon[xxxiv]

For one who trusts in God, his sustenance is assured to him no matter what may occur. As stated, "To make known to you that man does not live on bread alone, but man may live on anything God decrees" (Deuteronomy 8:3). It is also written, "Lions have been reduced to starvation; those who seek God will not lack any good" (Psalm 34:11). Also, "Fear God, you, His holy ones. Those who fear Him lack nothing" (ibid., 34:10).

Chovot HaLevavot[xxxv]

You, this generation,
See the word of God.
Have I been like a desert to Israel?
Like a land of deep gloom?
Jeremiah 2:31

During the days of Jeremiah, the prophet rebuked the people for abandoning the study of Torah to earn a livelihood. The people asked him, "If we leave our work and study Torah, how will we be sustained?" Jeremiah took the jar of manna from the Temple and declared, "See the word of God." He did not say, "Listen," but "See—it was with this that your ancestors were sustained in the desert. God has many messengers to prepare the needs of those who fear Him."
Rashi[xxxvi]

It is advisable to recite the passage of the manna (Exodus 16) every day. This will assist a person in believing that his needs are provided for him by God with individual providence. "The children of Israel did so; some gathered much, some gathered little. When they measured it on a scale, the one who gathered much was not better off and the one who gathered little had no deficiency: each had gathered exactly enough for each one to eat" (Exodus 16:17). This teaches that extra work does not help at all. It is stated in the Jerusalem Talmud, "One who recites the passage of the manna every day is assured to have sufficient food."
Mishnah Berurah

From the great and public miracles of the Bible a person can learn to count the hidden miracles, which are truly the foundation of the Torah. A person has no true share in the teaching of Moses until he believes that all of our life's events are all miraculous; there is no nature or custom that the world follows, whether for the masses or for the individual. Everything is a decree from God.

Ramban[xxxvii]

Who among you reveres God,
Listens to the voice of His servant?
Though he walk in darkness,
Has no light,
Let him trust in God's reputation,
And rely on his Master.
Isaiah 50:10

"Though he walk in darkness…"
Even if troubles come to you, trust in God's reputation
that He will save you.
Rashi

A person who regularly attends the house of worship and one day does not attend—God inquires about such a person. If they went to perform a good deed, then their choice was acceptable. But if they did not attend in order to pursue business, their choice was unacceptable. As the verse says, "Who among you reveres God, and listens to the voice of His servant?"; these usually attend the service. "Though he walk in darkness" (does not attend the house of worship), he "has no light" (since his reason for not attending was to pursue business). Therefore, "let him trust in God's reputation, and rely on his Master" and not go to pursue business at the time of prayer.
Talmud Bavli[xxxviii]

There are some people who may make a mistake in their thinking and reason this way, "By pursuing a living, I do a good deed, as it allows me to support my family." Therefore the Talmud teaches that a person should trust in God, Who will provide the needs of your house, and should not refrain from attending the house of worship.
Mahrasha

At the time of prayer there is no good deed that one should do other than attend the house of worship. How can a person think that he must work when he should be praying to God to provide for his needs? Only because such a person does not sufficiently trust in God.
Vilna Gaon[xxxix]

A faithful man will have many blessings,
One who hurries to become wealthy will
not go unpunished.
Proverbs 28:20

"A faithful man will have many blessings"—this refers to a person who conducts his business dealings faithfully. His investments will grow; the Holy One, blessed is He, will provide his income. Moreover, a faithful man is called righteous, as the verse says, "A righteous man lives by his faith" (Habakuk 2:4).
Rav Chaim Vital[xl]

A person must intensely concentrate when reciting Psalm 145. Our sages say that one who recites Psalm 145 three times a day is assured a place in the world to come. Especially, one must concentrate when saying the verse, "You open your hand, satisfying the desire of all living creatures" (Psalms 145:16). The main reason the sages instituted this psalm to be recited was for people to recite this verse, which contains the praise of God, who oversees all of His creation and provides their needs.

Tur[xli]

Satisfying the desire of all living creatures.
Psalm 145:16

It does not state "their sustenance," but "their desire." God grants each and every person his heart's request.
Midrash Rabbah Tehilim

A person should say, prior to any act or deed, whether it is important or insignificant, "If it is God's will."
Shelah HaKadosh[xlii]

One who works exceedingly hard will receive no benefit for his work if he does not combine his hard work with support from Heaven to achieve his request. Those who are beloved before Him achieve their requests with ease, without toil, and with minimal effort. This is what the psalmist intended when he said, "If God does not build the house, the laborers toil in vain. If God does not guard the city, the watchman keeps vigil in vain. It is vain, you who rise early and stay awake late, who eat the bread of sadness; He grants the same to His beloved ones in their sleep" (Psalm 127:12). Meaning—woe to you who wake up early and return late at night to your homes, only to eat your bread with sadness and concern. Your efforts are a waste if you do not request help from Heaven. If you were only beloved of Him, He would gladly grant your needs, with minimal effort, in the merit of trust you have in Him. You would have your needs with ease and sleep soundly. This is similar to the verse, "At one with peace, I lie down and sleep, for You alone sustain me" (Psalm 4:9).
Rabbi Avraham ben HaRambam[xliii]

A person needs some form of work, be what it may, in order to be able to stand on his own two feet and not need to travel from land to land. Seek shelter in God, and He will surely send blessings into the pursuits of your hands.

Such a person's reward is very great, in this world and in the world to come. "How abundant is the good You have in store for those who fear You; for those who take refuge in You" (Psalm 31:29).

There are two paths for trusting in God. The first is the type that people naturally understand: that a person work long hours and trust that God will assist him. The other path is when a person trusts so intensely in God that he does not pursue his business as others do. He does not travel to distant lands, even though everyone else in his city does. Others advise him to travel as well. Yet he does not travel since he does not want to diminish his time of study of Torah or his ability to perform good deeds. It is for this second path that the verse speaks of "How abundant is the good You have in store for those who fear You; for those who take refuge in You" (Psalms 31:29).
Kuntrus Nefusot Yisrael[xliv]

There is a story of a man who was studying during his set time for study. His friends approached him and said, "Come, let us go purchase some merchandise to sell." He responded, "I will not leave my time I have set aside for study to make money. If it is appropriate for me to have this money, God will provide it for me after I have finished studying."

Talmud Yerushalmi[xlv]

Our sages of blessed memory state, "If a person sees that his income is barely sufficient, he should give charity." The intent of this act is to demonstrate your trust in God with all your might and give charity with the little that remains to you. God knows the solutions to your problems better than you do. By demonstrating your trust in God with a full heart, believing that He will send His blessings to your empty house, you become a vessel ready to receive His endless blessings.

Or HaMeir[xlvi]

A righteous person eats to his heart's content;
The belly of the wicked is empty.
Proverbs 13:25

"A righteous person eats to his heart's content," since "a righteous man lives by his faith" (Habakkuk 2:4). Meaning, a righteous person eats until he is satisfied and is not concerned if there will be enough for tomorrow; he trusts that God will provide. The wicked, however, do not trust in God, and therefore eat less than their fill, hoping to save for the future: "The belly of the wicked is empty."
Mitsvat HaBitachon

Complete faith in God is considered one of the 613 commandments, as the verse states, "You must be completely with God your Lord" (Deuteronomy 18:13).
Sefer Haredim[xlvii]

Our sages have stated, "Desire removes a person from the world." Meaning, in this person's great desire for wealth he does not have sufficient time to study Torah or to fulfill the commandments. He denies God's providence, that all events are the result of His will. Similarly, our sages have stated, "Anyone who has bread in his basket and worries about what will be tomorrow has little faith." Yet to one who trusts in God, no higher spiritual level can be ascribed to such a person: "Happy are all who seek shelter in You" (Psalms 2:12).

Rav Chaim Vital[xlviii]

One who trusts in God will sprout salvation from his affliction; all of his troubles will be eased due to his trust. Yet he who trusts in his wealth will quickly fall from his honor and his comfort as a punishment for trusting in his money.
Rabbenu Yonah[xlix]

Trust in Time of Battle

If you think in your heart,
"These nations are mightier than I,
How will I be able to banish them?"
Do not be afraid of them.
Remember what God did for you
To Pharaoh and all of Egypt.
The wondrous acts you saw with your own eyes.
The signs, the demonstrations;
With His strong hand and His outstretched arm,
He took you out of Egypt.
So will God do to all the nations you fear.
Deuteronomy 7:17

A person should not fear other nations in battle. "When you go to war against your enemies and you see horses and chariots and a nation more numerous than you, do not fear them. God, who took you from the land of Egypt, is with you" (Deuteronomy 20:1). Additionally, "Whoever is afraid or disheartened, let him return home and not fight in battle, so the courage of his comrades does not wane as his has" (Deuteronomy 20:8). Since he has become afraid in seeing a large camp, and it is appropriate that he not be afraid at all (only trust in God) he is commanded to return back home so as to not make his friends afraid.

This is the meaning of the verse, "A man's fears become his trap" (Proverbs 29:25). Being afraid of other people is a sin, and it can cause one to fall into the grasp of his enemies. A person should not be afraid of other people at all. "He who trusts in God will be secure" (Proverbs 29:25), he will be saved from troubles in the merit of his trust. This is similar to what Isaiah taught: "What ails you that you fear men who will die, mortals who will become grass?" (Isaiah 51:12).
Rabbenu Bachya

Do not rebel against God,
Have no fear of the nation who dwells in the land:
They are no more than our bread,
Their protection has departed from them.
Have no fear of them!
Numbers 14:9

At that time, Hanani the seer came to King Asa of Judah and said, "Since you relied on the king of Aram and did not rely on your God, the army of Aram has slipped out of your hands. The Cushites and Libyans were a mighty army, with chariots and horsemen in very great numbers, yet you relied on God and He delivered them into your hands. For the eyes of God range over the entire earth, to support those who are wholeheartedly with Him. You have acted foolishly in this matter, and from now on you will be beset by wars."
2 Chronicles 16:7–9

It is clear from many sources in the writings of the prophets that a person's primary way of being saved from his enemies is dependent on the amount he trusts in God.
Machaneh Yisrael[li]

Joab said, "If the Arameans prove too strong for me, you come to my aid; if they are too strong for you, I will come to your aid. Let us be strong and resolute for the sake of our people and the cities of our God; God will do what He deems appropriate."
2 Samuel 10:11-12

Trust and Prayer

Rabbi Yochanan and Rabbi Elazar stated, "Even if a sharp sword is placed on a person's neck, he should not stop requesting mercy, as the verse states, 'Though He slay me, I will trust in Him'" (Job 13:15).

Rav Chanan stated, "Even if a dream interpreter tells a person that he will die tomorrow, do not stop requesting mercy. 'The majority of dreams are vanities and many words; rather, fear God'" (Ecclesiastes 5:6).
Talmud Bavli[lii]

Rav Chanan's statement applies to both of the above-mentioned situations. Even if a dream interpreter told you that you were to die, and a sharp sword was against your neck, still do not stop asking for mercy.
Iyun Yaakov

One who prays should not think that God will answer his prayer since he prayed well. Rather, he should think that God will answer him out of His great kindness.

Shulchan Arukh[liii]

If a person wants to pursue any business matter, prior to commencing his venture he should say, "with God's help." He should pray this short prayer, "Master of the Universe, in Your holy scriptures it is stated, 'One who trusts in God is surrounded by kindness,' and it is written, 'You sustain everything' (Psalm 32:10; Nehemiah 9:6). Grant me, from Your kindness, a blessing in the venture I am about to start."

If the venture is successful, the person should say, "I was successful with the help of God." If it did not do well, the person should reflect and consider the outcome as a result of his sins. He should search his conduct and find an area to improve—perhaps he forgot to return a sum of money or neglected to do a charitable act. He can then admit his error and correct his fault.

Shelah HaKadosh

Praying with Intent

One who prays must focus his heart on the meaning of each word as he says it. He should picture himself in the presence of God. He should remove all troubling thoughts until his mind is pure and he can focus on each word. If he were to beseech a mortal king, how much would he plan each word so as not to err? All the more so when one prays before the King of kings.

Shulchan Arukh[liv]

A person should pray in a supplicating manner, as a beggar standing by the door: gently. Do not conduct yourself as if your prayer was a burden that you sought to remove. *Ibid.*

"As a beggar standing by the door: gently. You should speak quietly as a person asking for mercy for himself. Consider that there is no being, angel, or force in the world that can grant your request. All is dependent on God's will.

"Do not conduct yourself as if your prayer was a burden that you sought to remove." Meaning, even if you are saying the prayer in a supplicating tone, yet you are not concentrating as if you are standing before the King, you are praying simply out of habit or because you feel obligated. This is not appropriate.

Do not think it is appropriate that God answer your prayer since you prayed with sincerity. This has the opposite effect; when a person calls attention to his merit, it also calls attention to his deficiencies. Rather, consider that God will answer your prayer out of His great compassion. *Mishnah Berurah, ibid.*

Our sages commented that prayer is called "service of the heart." A great amount of energy is required to focus our thoughts so they do not wander from place to place while praying. To intend our thoughts to be joyful and to attach ourselves to God, is a mighty service. A person must accustom himself to praying without any extraneous thoughts. Due to this great quantity of effort, our sages refer to prayer as "service of the heart."
Shelah

Prayer with Tears

Hear my prayer, God,
Give ear to my cry.
Do not be deaf to my tears.
Psalms 39:13

When I call out and plead,
He shuts out my prayer.
Lamentations 3:8

Rabbi Eliezer said, "From the day the temple was destroyed, the gates of prayer were closed, as Jeremiah said after the Temple was destroyed, 'When I call out and plead, He shuts out my prayer.' Yet the gates of prayer with tears were not closed: 'Do not be deaf to my tears.'"
Talmud Bavli[lv]

Since the verse in Psalms does not state "see my tears" but "do not be deaf to my tears," we can infer that God recognizes prayer offered with tears. We must only request that our prayers be accepted.
Rashi, ibid.

The whole city was saying that Esau would marry Leah, both being the oldest, and Jacob would marry Rachel, since they were the youngest. Leah would cry while praying, "May it be your will that I not fall into the lot of that wicked man." Rav Huna reflected, "See how powerful prayer is; not only did Leah not marry Esau, she married Jacob first!"
Midrash Rabbah

Prayer is best offered when one cries. Therefore the Psalmist said, "Hear my prayer, God, give ear to my cry. Do not be deaf to my tears" (Psalms 39:13). This happened to King Hezekiah: "Hezekiah wept profusely" (2 Kings 20:3). God's response to Hezekiah was, "I have heard your prayer; I have heard your tears" (2 Kings 20:4).

Similarly with Hannah: "Hannah prayed to God, weeping all the while" (1 Samuel 1:10).

Rabbenu Bachya[lvi]

Prayers during Health
and Illness

❧❦

Rabbi Isaac the son of Rabbi Judah said, "A person should always ask for mercy to not become sick, for if you become sick, the Heavenly Court will ask, 'What merit do you have to be healed?'"
Talmud Bavli[lvii]

Rabbi Elazar Ha-Kapar said, "A person should always ask for mercy to not become poor, since even if he does not become poor, his son or grandson may." The merit of this prayer will then be transferred to whichever of your descendants is in need.
Talmud Bavli[lviii]

Upon hearing good news, one should recite the blessing, "Blessed are you, God, Master of the Universe, who has kept us alive, sustained us, and brought us to this time." If the good news also benefits another, he should say, "Blessed are You, God, Master of the Universe, Who is good and does good."

Upon hearing bad news, one should recite the blessing, "Blessed are You, God, Master of the Universe, Who is the true judge."

A person is obligated to recite the blessing with a complete agreement in mind and soul as if he were blessing God for some joyous, good occasion; difficult occasions for servants of God can be their joy and their good. By accepting with love that which was decreed upon them, their bad circumstance is an opportunity to serve God, which is their highest pleasure.
Shulchan Arukh[lix]

"As if he were blessing…" In truth, all afflictions, whether bodily or monetarily, are a means of atonement for past sins. This punishment removes the need for further afflictions in the world to come, for there the punishment will be much greater.

It is recorded in the Midrash, "Isaac asked for afflictions." (For he recognized how great the punishments would be in the future. …) God responded, 'Indeed, you have asked well. With you I will start,' and that is the meaning of the verse, "It was as Isaac became old, his eyesight dimmed" (Genesis 27:1).
Mishnah Berurah ibid.

Before going to a doctor, one should recite the following prayer:

"Master of the Universe, I believe with a complete faith that my cure is in Your hands, and it is not the doctor who has the ability to cure me. May it be Your will, God, and God of my ancestors, that You grant me a complete recovery. Assist me to know that this doctor I am choosing to see will be a faithful messenger from You to give me the proper medications, so I can be healed in order to be healthy and strong to serve You and to study with no ulterior motive."
Eved HaMelech

A person who goes to have any procedure or eat any food for health should recite the following prayer:
"May it be Your will, my God and God of my ancestors, that this act should serve to heal me, as You are a beneficent healer."
Shulchan Arukh [lx]

Do not think that there is any way of being healed other than through God's will. While reciting this prayer, place your trust in God, and ask that He heal you.
Mishnah Berurah ibid.

Another prayer:

"Master of the Universe! I know that in Your judgment You have afflicted me, for my own good, to atone for my sins. I do not object to these afflictions. On the contrary, I am pleased with them; I will accept them lovingly. Yet I am deeply pained for how these sufferings have minimized my ability to serve You.

"Therefore, I am prepared to take treatments so my body can be healthy and strong to serve You. You grant doctors permission to heal, as You have told the sages of Israel. Yet, my eyes turn toward You, as I know that my health is in Your hands. Therefore I recite my supplication to You. Heal me completely, along with all the sick of Israel Your nation, a healing of the body and healing of the soul, since You are God, a King who is a faithful and merciful healer.

"Answer me, God. Answer me. Do not approach Your servant in justice; do not let Your mercy depart from me. Your kindness and truth always support me. God, please heal me, along with the rest of the ill of Israel. Do so for Your name; do so for the power of Your right hand, for the sake of Your Torah, for the sake of Your beloved ones. May your right hand save and respond to me. May the words of my mouth and meditations of my heart be pleasing before You, God, my rock and redeemer."
Pele Yo'etz

A Doctor's Prayer

Master of the Universe, You alone are God. You made the heavens and all the celestial beings, the earth and all that is on it, the sea and all that is within it. You sustain all life; the heavens bow to You. There is no being above or below that can instruct You what to do. You formed man from dust and blew a living soul into him. If he merits to do Your will, man has dominion over all You have created. If not, he is afflicted with suffering and illness, "he is reproached by pains on his bed; the trembling of his bones is constant" (Job 33:19).

You are the faithful healer: "I have struck and I heal" (Deuteronomy, 32:39); "He gave an order and healed them; He delivered them from death" (Psalm 107:20). You do this to make known to all who live that You are the healer, that complete dominion and power belong to You. You oversee all people, and every detail of their lives. You created medicines to heal people, and You have commanded doctors to use them to heal: "The healer will heal" (Exodus 21:19).

You, in Your great compassion, have made me merit to know a small portion of the wisdom of healing. To do Your will, my God, is my desire. "Do not withhold good from one who deserves it, since you have the power to do it for him" (Proverbs 3:27). On my deepest level, I want to practice the craft of healing with Your help, since you are the healer, not I.

I am like clay in the hands of the artist. I will not rely on my wisdom, nor will I place my trust in the medications.

They are all messengers to fulfill Your will, and to tell of Your greatness and Your providence.

Practicing medicine is exceedingly dangerous. I am fearful that I may err, like a blind man in darkness. I am ignorant, without understanding. May it be Your will, my God and God of my ancestors, that You grant me sound intelligence, knowledge, and understanding. Enlighten my eyes to understand, to recognize illnesses of the body. Teach me the correct medicines to heal; save me from stumbling. Pour Your kindness on me, so I can heal the souls of Your people.

If a deathly ill person, whose time has nearly come, should appear before me for treatment, may it be Your will that I not hasten his death, even by a moment. Teach me to give him the proper medications until his time comes. If he dies, may it be Your will that people not suspect me, and not murmur that I was the cause of his death. Let them judge me righteously and agree that it was the decree of the King who has in His possession the soul of all living, and the spirit of all of humanity.

If his time has not come, yet You are afflicting him with pains in Your great mercy, so that he may repent completely, since You do not desire death, but that people should repent from their ways and live, may it be Your will that I may know what to say, have merit to guide the man to accept his sufferings with love, that they should be an atonement for his sins.

Please God, save me from contentions, and that I should not be jealous of others, nor should others be jealous of me. Rather, let love, friendship, and peace dwell between me and all other doctors.

Grant me grace, kindness, and compassion in Your eyes, and in the eyes of all who see me. May I do what You have commanded me to do to all ill people.

My Father in Heaven, strengthen, please, my faculty of memory. If an illness should come before me, help me to remember quickly the appropriate medication if I have learned it. If I have not learned which medication to administer, help me to learn it, either by finding a book of medications, or perhaps there will be some discovery among doctors that I should merit to learn, and heal the illness. You are the one who affects all causes.

My Father in Heaven, may I always merit to cause good, and never bad. May no damage come from me, not death or any damage even to one limb.

My Father in Heaven, open my eyes that I may gaze on the secrets of Your creation and apply the correct medications, and share my findings with all, that I may tell everyone of Your majesty.

May it be Your will, my Father in Heaven, that You send blessings to all of my endeavors. May my finances be blessed, and may I be able to do good deeds. My sustenance and the sustenance of my family is dependent on Your control and not the control of mortals. May it be given with plenty, and not constricted. May I not need to take payment from ill people who are in poverty. On the contrary, may I be able to provide for them. If people honor me because of my wisdom, may it not lead me to be haughty. May I always be humble. Save me from any evil inclination. Love me and hear my prayer, as You hear the prayer of every lip.

Margilot Tovot LeMahari Tzhalon

Prayers for Traveling

Prayer for Travel

May it be Your will, my God and God of my ancestors, that
You guide me in peace, support me in peace, lead me in
peace, and lead me to find my desires with life, happiness,
and peace. Save me from any enemy, robber, or wild
animals, and from all kinds of trouble that frequently
occur. Send blessings into all the works of my hands. Grant
me grace, kindness, and compassion in Your eyes and in
the eyes of all who see me. Listen to my prayers. You are
God, who listens to prayers and supplications. Blessed are
You, God, who listens to prayers.

Prayer for a Sea Voyage

May it be Your will, our Father in Heaven, that you protect us from dangerous waves, a turbulent wind, from trouble and pain. Bring a beneficent wind from Your storehouse to guide the ship. Strengthen the captains and the workers to guide the ship appropriately. May we reach our desires with life and peace, without any trouble or damage; in You alone we trust. Guard my soul and save me, for in You I find shelter. We will praise God from now and forevermore. Praise God!

Prayer when Traveling on an Airplane

May it be Your will, owner of heaven and earth, that our plane fly in peace. Save us from dangerous turbulence, from dangerous moments that frequently occur in the skies. Save us from the hand of all enemies and wicked men, and from every trouble and damage. Guide the pilots to direct the plane appropriately. May we reach our desires with life and peace, without any trouble or damage; in You alone we trust. Guard my soul and save me, for in You I find shelter. We will praise God from now and forevermore. Praise God!

Glossary

The world to come—loosely used to refer to the afterlife. Exactly what this time period will be is a matter of debate that is addressed in a variety of primary and secondary sources. For our purposes, it is life after this temporal world. The intent in this context is that suffering in this world is better than suffering in the world to come.

613 commandments—There is a rabbinic tradition that there are 613 commandments (in Hebrew, *Mitzvoth*). Many laws may be included in fulfilling one commandment. Yet, the term has become used as a way of referring in general to God's expectations for the Jewish people.

Torah—technically refers to the Five Books of Moses, also known as the Pentateuch. More generally, the term can refer to any study of Judaic texts.

Selected Bibliography

Berachot—a tractate from the Babylonian Talmud, compiled circa 500 CE. The Talmud is a collection of laws and ethical teachings and is the backbone of Jewish tradition.

Biur HaGra Mishlei (explanations of the Gra on Proverbs)—see Vilna Gaon.

Chovot HaLevavot (Duties of the Heart)—a profound ethical work written by Rabbenu Bachya ibn Paquda in Spain at the end of the eleventh century.

Emreh Noam (Pleasant Sayings) —see Vilna Gaon.

Eved HaMelech—commentary on selected Biblical texts by Rabbi Shemuel Houminer, 1914–1978.

Iyun Yaakov (Analyzing Yaakov)—commentaries on the classic work Eyn Yaakov, a collection of Talmudic passages dealing with ethical teachings. *Iyun Yaakov* was authored by Rabbi Yaakov Reiser, 1661–1733, in Prague.

Kol Eliyahu Hachadash (The New Voice of Eliyahu)—see Vilna Gaon.

Maggid Mezritch (Teacher from Mezritch)—Rabbi Dov Baer of Mezritch, foremost student of the founder of the Chassidic Movement, the Baal Shem Tov. He consolidated the nascent Chassidic movement.

Maharil, Netiv HaBitachon (The Path of Trust)—*Maharil* is a Hebrew acronym for "Our Teacher, the Rabbi, Yaakov Levi." Rabbi Jacob Moelin lived c. 1365–1427 in Germany.

Mahrasha—abbreviation for the Hebrew of Morenu HaRav Shmuel Eliezer. Rabbi Shmuel Eliezer Aidel lived in Poland 1555–1631. He was one of the most important rabbis of his time; his commentaries are reprinted on nearly all editions of the Talmud.

Malbim—Rabbi Meir Leibush, known by the acronym for his full name. He lived from 1809–1879 in various European cities.

Meiri—Menachem ben Shlomo, 1249–1316. He lived in Provence.

Midrash—a generic term denoting the moral and ethical traditions and explanations of the rabbis of the Talmudic era. In the years following the compilation of the Talmud, around 500 CE, much of this material was collected into texts known as Midrashim. In the present book, many times the title *Midrash* is followed by the name of a text that it is commenting on, such as *Tehilim* (Psalms) or *Mishleh* (Proverbs).

Midrash HaGadol—a Midrashic collection written by Rabbi David ben Amram Adani, circa 1250. It was used extensively by the Yemenite community.

Mishneh Berurah—a commentary on *Orach Chaim,* the first section of the *Shulchan Arukh* (see below). It was written by Rabbi Israel Meir Kagan, better known as the Chofetz Chaim, Poland 1838–1933. It has become one of the most widely accepted modern legal works.

Mitsvat HaBitachon—a collection of teachings on faith from the Jewish tradition, collected by Rabbi Shemuel Houminer, Jerusalem 1914–1977.

Ohr HaMeir—written by Rabbi Meir Shapiro of Lublin 1887–1933.

Orchot Tzadikim, Shaar HaSimcha (The Way of the Righteous, the Gate of Joy)—one of the earliest works on ethical and moral self-improvement. It was written in the eleventh century by an unknown author.

Pele Yo'etz—written by Rabbi Eliezer Papo. He was born in Sarajevo and lived from 1785–1826.

Rabbi Avraham ben HaRambam son of the Rambam (Hebrew acronym for Rabbi Moses son of Maimon—in English known as Maimonides). Rabbi Avraham took over his father's position as leader of the Egyptian community and as the court physician at the age of eighteen. *HaMaspik LeOvedeh Hashem (A Guide for the Servants of God)* is a classic devotional text.

Rabbenu Bachya ben Asher—Biblical commentator who lived during the thirteenth century in Spain. He also wrote an encyclopedia on moral and ethical topics called *Kad HaKemach (The Jar of Flour)*. The phrase is a reference to the jar of flour that miraculously sustains the women in 1 Kings 17:14. His encyclopedia is also intended to sustain the Jewish people's basic needs.

Rabbenu Yonah—a thirteenth century master of Jewish ethics. He wrote commentaries on many Biblical and rabbinic texts that are widely studied today.

Ramban—Rabbi Moses son of Nachman, known as Nachmanides, 1194–c. 1270. He lived in Catalan, Spain, and was exiled after debating the apostate Pablo Christiani at the request of King James I of Aragon in 1263. He moved to Israel where he began to rebuild the settlement there for the remainder of his years. He wrote extensively on the Talmud, Bible, and other philosophical works. His work, *HaEmunah VeHaBitachon (Faith and Trust)* is a classic in how to understand Judaism's views on these subjects and is often quoted in this text.

Rashi—an acronym for Rabbi Shlomo Yitzchaki. He lived in Troyes, France, from 1040–1105. His commentary on the Bible and Talmud are indispensable tools for understanding Judaism's most important primary texts. His comments often reveal or clarify a deeper meaning of the text.

Rav Chaim Vital—Rabbi Chaim Vital was the main student of the foremost Kabbalist, Rabbi Isaac Luria, also known as the Arizal. He lived from 1543–1620 in Israel. Rabbi Vital is responsible for recording most of the Arizal's teachings.

Shabbat—a tractate from the Babylonian Talmud, compiled circa 500 CE. The Talmud is a collection of laws and ethical teachings and is the backbone of Jewish tradition.

Shaar HaBitachon (The Gate of Trust)—authored by Rabbenu Bachya ibn Paquda in Spain at the end of the eleventh century.

Sefer Haredim (Book of the Awestruck)—written by Rabbi Eliezer Azkari circa 1550.

Sefer ha-Ikkarim (Book of Principals)—written by Rabbi Joseph Albo c. 1380–1444 in Spain. It is considered a classic work on the fundamentals of Judaism.

Shelah HaKadosh (The Holy Shelah)—a title derived from the author Rabbi Isaiah Horowitz's most famous work, *Shnei Luchot HaBrit (Two Tablets of the Covenant)*. He was born in Prague in 1565 and died in Safed in 1630. The work had a tremendous impact on Jewish thought.

Shulchan Arukh (lit. *Set Table*)—authored by Rabbi Yosef Cairo, 1488–1575, in Safed, Israel. The *Shulchan Arukh* is the standard code of Jewish law. It follows the division of the earlier Halachic code the *Arbah Turim*, see *Tur*. In the present book, two of those sections are quoted: *Orach Chaim (The Way of Life)* and *Yoreh De'ah (Teaching Knowledge)*.

Talmud Bavli—compiled circa 500 CE in Babylonia. The Talmud is a collection of laws and ethical teachings and is the backbone of Jewish tradition. Since this compilation was written later than the Jerusalem Talmud, and since it is more extensive, it is considered more authoritative on legal matters.

Talmud Yerushalmi—Jerusalem Talmud, compiled c. 350–400 C.E. It contains more laws relating to agriculture than the Babylonian Talmud.

Tur—short for *Arbah Turim*, written by Rabbi Yaakov ben Asher in Spain, 1270–1340. Rabbi Asher was the first rabbi to divide Jewish Law that is applicable in our times, without the Temple in Jerusalem, into four sections. This division helps to simplify the study of Jewish Law.

Turei Zahav (Rows of Gold)—written by Rabbi David HaLevi Segal, 1586–1667, who lived mostly in Poland. The work is an indispensable commentary on the *Shulchan Arukh*.

Unkolus—a convert to Judaism during the Talmudic era, c. 35–120 CE. According to tradition, he authored one of the first translations of the Bible into Aramaic.

Vilna Gaon—Rabbi Eliyahu of Vilna, also known as the Gra (an acronym for the Hebrew Gaon Rabbi Eliyahu). *Gaon* is a title reserved for a master in Jewish traditions and texts.

Yalkut Shimoni—A collection of interpretations on the Bible.

Zohar (Book of Splendor)— a work on Jewish mysticism. It is the classic text of Kabbalah, from the school of Rabbi Shimon Bar Yochai, and written by his student Rabbi Akiva in the second century. It was written as a commentary on the Hebrew Bible.

i   The complete book was translated for an observant Jewish audience under the title *Faith and Trust* by Kalmen Gross and Dovid Rossoff published by Quantum Press and distributed by Feldheim. Many of the teachings contained in the original require a background in Judaic texts; I have attempted to select and translate parts of the work for a reader with no background in Judaic texts to be able to appreciate these teachings. I have sought to offer a translation into modern and poetic language, which at times is different than how many of these verses and teachings have previously been translated. I have also included other sources not included in the original Hebrew text.

ii   The complete Hebrew text and translation can be obtained from Feldheim publishers.

iii   Rabbi Judah Lew, often referred to by his acronym of his Hebrew name, Maharal (Prague, 1525–1609), quotes his grandfather, who stated that it is an ancient custom to recite these verses of trust to bring blessing or to help a person prior to entering into a business venture. I have found this collection a source of inspiration in happy times and consolation in difficult moments.

This translation is my own original work. I have drawn extensively from two translations of the Bible, the Jewish Publication Society's and the Artscroll translation. However, my intent here is to offer an authentic translation based in Jewish sources that is poetic and lucid. The Artscroll translation attempts to be true to the original text at the expense of ease of reading in English; the JPS translation translates into modern English idiom, often softening the poetic nature of the text. Therefore, I offer translations that are often based on classic Jewish tradition. Two authorities, Unkolus and the Malbim, were great resources for me. Their translation/explanation may veer from the plain meaning of the text, yet offers a more satisfactory devotional prayer.

I have also translated for the modern audience. I therefore do not frequently use the title "Lord" although it may be more accurate to differentiate between the use of "Lord" and "God." I also use the word should rather than shall.

iv This is the first of many references to God being more present for one group or individual than for others. This theme is extended to God's protection from enemies, persecutors, etc. Are these real enemies or metaphors for something else? King David did live a highly dangerous life: he was often in battle and had many political enemies. Yet I find these verses more relevant to my life and to my conception of God—a God who is "Good to all; His compassion is for all His works" (Psalms 145:9) —to think of these enemies as the forces in life or in my own personality that take me away from serving God as I truly desire. My anger, my laziness, my yearning for pleasure, and my imagined limitations are all elements that can be victorious over my most important battles fought in my mind. It is these enemies I know God will help me fight against. It is this metaphor I employ whenever I encounter this expression.

v May refer to the declaration above, "God is the stronghold of my life." Alternatively, it may refer to the following verse. The meaning would then be expressing confidence in God's protection since the psalmist has always sought only to "live in the house of God all the days of my life."

vi   Proverbs 3

vii   *Kad HaKemach, Bitachon*

viii   *Mamar Revii,* 46.

ix   49

x   *Kol Eliyahu Hachadash*

xi   *HaEmunah VeHaBitachon* Chapter 1

xii   *Mamar revii* 45

xiii   47

xiv   48

xv   Page 34 in original Hebrew edition, 19 in Feldheim edition.

xvi   Page 34 in original Hebrew edition, 19 in Feldheim edition.

xvii   *Lekutai Yikarim* 207

xviii   *Behar* 110

xix   *HaEmunah VeHaBitachon* Chapter 1

xx   *Tehilim* Psalm 31

xxi   *Kad HaKemach, Reshut*

xxii   *Mishlei* 16:20

xxiii   *Shaar HaBitachon* Chapter 5

xxiv   First quote in this section in both editions.

xxv   *Parshat Shelach*

xxvi   *Vayeshev* 40:23

xxvii   *Kad HaKemach, Bitachon*

xxviii *Shaar HaSimcha*

xxix   *Vayakel* 198

xxx   *Biur HaGra, Mishlei*

xxxi   *Mishlei*

xxxii   *Shaar HaBitachon* Chapter 4

xxxiii   *Yoreh Deah* 336:1

About the Author

Jeffrey Alhadeff studied in Israel prior to earning his master's in liberal arts from Johns Hopkins University and a second master's in Talmudic Law from Ner Israel Rabbinical College. Currently, he is a Judaic Studies educator at Seattle Hebrew Academy and lives with his wife and children in Seattle, Washington.

1697862

Made in the USA